Questions
and
Answers

This edition published in 2008 by Arcturus Publishing Limited
26/27 Bickels Yard, 151–153 Bermondsey Street,
London SE1 3HA

Copyright © 2007 Arcturus Publishing Limited

ISBN: 978-1-84193-780-9

Printed in China

Design & Illustration by quadrum■

Questions and Answers

Capella

Contents

Q. What are bonobos?

A. Bonobos are a species of chimpanzee, discovered in 1928 by American scientist Horold Coolidge. They are our closest relatives in the animal kingdom, as they also walk upright on their feet. Some bonobos in captivity have even learned to speak a human language! Unlike other apes, a bonobo society is controlled by a female.

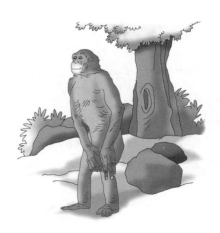

Q. Why are monkeys called social animals?

A. Most species of monkeys live in groups. The size of a group depends on how much food is available and if there are predators around.

Q. Why are howler monkeys unusual?

A. Howler monkeys make a peculiar barking sound. They can be heard up to 3 kilometres (1.9 miles) away.

Q. What do cats use their tongues for?

A. A cat's tongue is rough and covered with sharp, hook-like projections called papillae. Cats use their tongues to clean the flesh from the bones of their prey and to groom themselves.

Q. Are white tigers albinos?

A. White tigers are not albinos. White tigers have prominent stripes, but a true albino would have no stripes at all. White tigers are not a separate species, just differently colored members of the same species.

Q. Which is the smallest bear in the world?

A. Sun bears are the smallest of all bear species. Even then, they grow up to 1.5 metres (5 feet) in length and weigh up to 66 kilograms (146 pounds).

Q. How do you know when a bear is angry?

A. When threatened or agitated, bears stand up on their hind legs. They probably do this to appear larger to their enemies. They also use their clawed paws to slash at an attacker.

Q. Which is the fastest canine in the world?

A. Greyhounds are the fastest canines in the world. They have been known to run at speeds of up to 70 kilometres per hour (44 miles per hour)! African hunting dogs are also very fast and can maintain speeds of 50–60 kilometres per hour (31–37 miles per hour) for very long distances while chasing prey.

Q. What is a fennec?

A. Fennecs are the smallest canines. These small foxes are only 65 centimetres (2 feet) long from the top of their ears to the tip of their tails, and weigh less than 1.5 kilograms (3.3 pounds). These desert animals have oversized ears that help them to dispel excess heat from their body.

Q. Do elephants eat a lot?

A. The elephant's digestive system is very weak. It can digest only 40 per cent of the food it eats. It has to make up for this by eating a great deal. An adult eats about 140–270 kilograms (300–600 pounds) of leaves and grass every day.

Q. How big are the tusks of an elephant?

A. An African elephant's tusks are between 1.8–2.4 metres (6–8 feet) in length and weigh about 20–45 kilograms (50–100 pounds). Those of an Asian male are only about 1.5 metres (5 feet) in length and weigh about 30 kilograms (70 pounds).

Q. Do fish look after their eggs?

A. Most fish lay their eggs and then swim away. But not the sunfish; they make very caring parents. The male sunfish actully guards the female's eggs until they hatch. This is unlike other fish.

Q. Do fish go to sleep?

A. Some fish enjoy a nap. All members of the parrotfish family sleep at night. They make a bed out of their own saliva that covers them fully. Then they go to sleep on the sea floor. But most other types of fish continue to swim slowly even when they are resting, so it's difficult to tell if they have gone to sleep.

Q. How can deep sea fish see in the dark?

A. Fish that live in the deepest part of the oceans are bioluminescent, meaning they glow in the dark. Certain chemicals in the body of these fish produce a glowing light that helps them find their way through the dark waters. They also have large eyes and feelers, which help them to locate prey. In fact, it is because of these glowing fish that the deepest part of the ocean is known as the 'twilight zone'.

Q. How do pufferfish get their name?

A. Pufferfish defend themselves by puffing their bodies up with water until they are round and look much bigger and more scary than they actually are.

Q. Is size enough to scare an enemy off?

A. When size isn't enough to defend itself, the pufferfish uses poison. The poison, tetrodotoxin, is also found in the blue-ringed pufferfish and is 1,200 times stronger than cyanide. Pufferfish poison can kill 30 people!

Q. What do whales use their tails for?

A. The tail of a whale is divided into two parts, called flukes. While fish move their tails sideways to swim, whales swim by moving their flukes up and down in the water.

Q. Which is the largest whale in the world?

A. Blue whales are not only the largest whales, but also the largest animals ever to live on Earth. They can be as long as 34 metres (112 feet). They are also the loudest animals on Earth – 1.5 times as loud as a pneumatic drill. But they use such a low frequency to call one another that we cannot hear them.

Q. What is blubber?

A. Blubber is a layer of fat found between the skin and flesh of all whales. It preserves body heat as well as keeping whales afloat and storing energy.

Q. Are all sharks aggressive?

A. No. The horn shark, which is 1.2 metres (4 feet) long, hides under rocks during the day and comes out at night. It is a timid shark that eats only small fish and crustaceans.

Q. Do sharks ever attack whales?

A. The cookie-cutter shark attaches itself to a whale and then bites out a bit of its flesh with its razor-sharp teeth.

Q. How long do sharks normally live?

A. Sharks can live for many years. The great white shark can live for up to one hundred years!

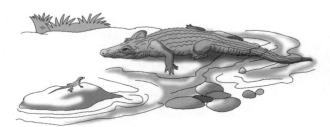

Q. Which are the largest and the smallest reptiles?

A. The estuarine crocodile is more than 7 metres (23 feet) long. The smallest reptile is the British Virgin Islands Gecko. It is just 18 millimetres (0.7 inches) long.

Q. Can I outrun a reptile?

A. A tortoise may be very slow on land but some reptiles are very fast. The spiny-tailed iguana can run at 35 kilometres per hour (21 miles per hour). You'd have to run quickly to beat it!

Q. Which snake is the fastest in the world?

A. The black mamba found in Africa can travel at speeds of 19 kilometres per hour (11.8 miles per hour.) This makes it the fastest snake in the world.

Q. Which is the longest snake in the world?

A. The reticulated python is the longest snake in the world. An adult reticulated python can grow up to 10 metres (33 feet) in length.

Q. Which is the most venomous snake in the world?

A. The inland taipan, a venomous snake found in Australia, is the most venomous snake in the world. Its venom is 400 times more powerful than the venom of a rattlesnake. Cobras, however, kill more people, because they live near populated areas.

Q. How does the spitting cobra get its name?

A. When threatened, spitting cobras spray venom into the eyes of the enemy, causing temporary blindness. This gives the snake enough time to escape. Spitting cobras have been known to spit venom to distances of about 2.5 metres (8 feet)!

Q. Is it true that boas and pythons can go without food for several days?

A. After a big meal, boas and pythons do not eat for several days. This is because the digestive juices in the snake's stomach take a long time to break down the food.

Q. Which is the smallest crocodile?

A. The dwarf crocodile is exceptionally small. Adult dwarf crocodiles do not grow to more than 2 metres (6.5 feet) in length.

Q. Which is the largest crocodile species?

A. The saltwater crocodile is not only the largest of all crocodiles, but also the largest reptile in the world. This huge reptile can be more than 6 metres (20 feet) in length and weigh over 1,500 kilograms (3,307 pounds).

Q. Why do some frogs and almost all toads secrete poison?

A. Frogs and toads secrete poison for safety. Most poison-arrow frogs and mantella frogs are brightly colored to warn their enemies. Some harmless frogs copy this coloring to protect themselves from predators who mistake them as poisonous!

Q. How long have insects been around?

A. One insect fossil, found in Russia, dates back to more than 100 million years before the first dinosaurs. Cockroaches are also older than dinosaurs.

Q. How many insects am I standing on?

A. If you are in a field, there could be dozens of insects under your feet. One acre can be home to more than 400,000,000 insects. 100,000,000 collembola (springtails) can live in a square metre.

Q. Can I eat an insect?

A. Some insects can be poisonous. However, in certain parts of the world people do eat non-harmful insects, such as ants, crickets and grasshoppers, since they are a cheap source of protein. But they have to be cooked in a certain way before they are safe to be eaten.

Q. Seabirds eat a lot of salt. Is this good for them?

A. Seabirds have salt glands on their face that excrete some of the salt they take in. But the salt does not seem to harm the birds – seabirds live longer than other types of birds. In fact, the albatross can live for up to 60 years.

Q. Which is the smallest flightless bird?

A. The Inaccessible Island rail of the South Atlantic is the world's smallest flightless bird. It is no more than 17 centimetres (2 inches) and weighs less than 30 grams (1 ounce).

Q. What do kiwis use their beaks for?

A. Kiwis have nostrils at the end of their long beaks. They thrust their beaks into the ground in search of food.

Q. Was there ever a flightless bird that was larger than the ostrich?

A. The aepyornis that lived on the island of Madagascar was the largest bird ever to live on this planet. It was more than 3 metres (10 feet) tall and weighed about 500 kilograms (1,100 pounds).

Q. How does a bee become queen of the colony?

A. Worker bees produce royal jelly. When a bee larva is fed a diet of royal jelly, it grows into a queen bee. All the others in the colony are fed royal jelly only for about two days. Then, they are given pollen and nectar or honey instead.

Art and Culture

Q. What is the world's most popular monument?

A. The Eiffel Tower is the most visited monument in the world with six and a half million visitors a year. It has had 200 million visitors since it was built.

Q. What is earth art?

A. In the 1960s and 1970s, artists like Robert Smithson used bulldozers instead of brushes to create art from natural materials. These works were called earth art. The earth art movement was influenced by concerns about the deterioration of the environment through pollution and deforestation.

Q. What is Minimalism?

A. In the 1950s, Frank Stella of the United States painted white pinstripes on a black canvas and called it 'The Marriage of Reason and Squalo'. When asked what it meant, he said "What you see is what you see". This style, where painted objects are not a symbol for anything else, is Minimalism.

Q. Where was the first skyscraper built?

A. It was built in Chicago in 1890, by Major William Le Baron Jenney and Louis Sullivan. It had ten floors and was used as the Home Insurance Building.

Q. Why is the Parthenon famous?

A. The Parthenon was a temple for the Greek goddess Athena. It was built between 447 and 433 BC and still stands at the Acropolis in Athens. Its decorative sculptures made of white marble make it an example of the best Grecian architecture.

Q. What is Stonehenge?

A. Stonehenge, built between 3000 and 1500 BC, is the best-known prehistoric stone structure in England. It was formed from tall standing stones, or megaliths, set in a circle within even older earthworks. UNESCO has declared it a World Heritage Site.

Q. What were the first musical instruments?

A. The earliest musical instruments were percussion instruments that kept a beat. These were made of material which the ancient man found easily, such as stones, branches and animal bones.

Q. Are some musical instruments really made of vegetables?

A. Yes. Traditional flutes are made of reeds and bamboo. Gourds and coconuts are dried to make various string instruments, as well as drums and castanets.

Q. What is pop art?

A. In the 1960s, American painters like Andy Warhol and Roy Lichtenstein created art from everyday objects. They used soup cans, comic books and advertisements to comment on modern life.

Q. What is pop music?

A. Pop is short for 'popular'. Popular music includes music from films and TV with lyrics often about everyday subjects.

Q. Which is the longest running musical?

A. The Broadway musical 'A Chorus Line' was performed for the last and 6,137th time on 28 April 1990 at the Shubert Theatre.

Q. What is classical music?

A. Western classical music was composed between the mid-1700s and the early 1800s in Europe. One of the most famous composers of this music was Wolfgang Amadeus Mozart.

Q. When did Western theatre begin?

A. Western theatre was developed in ancient Greece. It developed from a state festival in Athens, honoring the god Dionysus. Greek theatre is mostly famous for its tragic plays.

Q. What is Japanese Noh theatre?

A. Noh is a major form of classical Japanese musical drama that has been performed since the 14th century. Noh is unique in its slow, graceful movements and its use of distinctive masks.

Q. Why are some plays staged again and again?

A. Some plays are so popular that many people want to see them. 'Life with Father' by Clarence Day Jr. was staged in the USA about 3,200 times and 'Oklahoma!' by Richard Rodgers and Oscar Hammerstein had 2,000 performances.

Q. Did European theatre allow women performers?

A. No. Acting was considered disgraceful for women, so even Shakespeare's plays had young boys playing the parts of women. Women started acting in the seventeenth century.

Q. What is African theatre about?

A. In Africa, traditional theatre is often not written, but memorized. In Nigeria, the story of Obatala, the Nigerian creator god, is played every year. Entire villages participate in the play.

Q. When was the first movie camera invented?

A. The first hand-held camera was invented by the Lumiére brothers in France in 1895.

Q. What is a blockbuster film?

A. A blockbuster is a very popular film that generates huge revenues. 'Jaws' was the first film to earn more than $100 million. A mechanical monster shark was the hero.

Q. What are science fiction fantasy movies?

A. Science fiction or 'sci-fi' films are those that deal with an imagined scenario, unreal scientific discoveries or beings from outer space. 'Star Wars', directed by George Luas in 1977, is a classic sci-fi movie.

Q. When was the first Olympic Games held?

A. The original Olympic Games began in 776 BC, in Olympia in Greece and were held until 393 AD. Only in 1896 did the games begin again after a campaign by a French baron named Pierre Frédy.

Q. Have we learned any sports from other countries?

A. Many popular sports have been learned from other countries. In 1778, Captain Cook found the people of Hawaii surfing. Native Americans played games like lacrosse. The Mayans and Aztecs played ballgames in a court, which inspired basketball.

Q. What are team sports?

A. Sports played in a group or team, where two teams compete, are called team sports. Team sports like hockey, football, baseball, basketball and volleyball are played with a ball. In cricket and baseball, a bat is used to hit the ball, whereas in hockey, sticks are used.

Q. **What does 'track and field' mean?**

A. All running events, hurdles and speed walking are track and field sports, as are jumping and throwing events like shot-put, discus and javelin. Also included are cross-country runs, marathon and steeplechase, which has a water barrier in its 3,000-metre course.

Q. **Which is the oldest religion in the world still practiced?**

A. Hinduism began before 1500 BC and is still practised today.

Q. **What is the most popular religion in the world?**

A. Christianity is practiced in every continent where humans live. There are over 1.9 billion Christians who follow the teachings of Jesus Christ, who lived about 2000 years ago.

Q. Who are the Amish?

A. The Amish are a Christian sect known for their shunning of modern technology. The Amish, who live in the United States and in Ontario (Canada), avoid the use of electricity and cars as far as possible. They do not join the military, nor do they take any money from any government. They place a high value on humility, and disagree with vanity and pride.

Q. What is the meaning of 'Zoroastrianism'?

A. Zoroastrianism is a religion founded in Persia around the sixth century BC by the prophet Zarathushtra. Arabs later banned the religion. Zoroastrians or Parsees fled to India. Zoroastrianism believes in one god, Ahura Mazda. Their holy book is the Avesta.

Q. What were the earliest paintings about?

A. The earliest paintings were about things people did every day like hunting, and about the wild animals they saw. Horses, bison, deer and even human hands were drawn. These paintings were often made with pieces of colored stone. The painters were probably holy men or shamans.

Q. How did cinema begin?

A. In the early nineteenth century, scientists noticed that if a series of still pictures is made to move, it seems as if the image is moving naturally. This moving picture is what developed into movies, also known as motion pictures or films.

Q. Which was the first real entertainment movie to be shown?

A. In 1901 American projectionist Edwin S. Porter began making films that told a story. 'The Great Train Robbery', made in 1903, was the first film shown for entertainment. Nickelodeon theatres sprung up in converted storefronts and charged 5 cents for a show.

Q. When did sound come in?

A. Recorded sound was used in the late 1920s. Within five years, sound was used in almost every film. Once sound could be recorded, musical films became popular. Warner Brothers made films which featured large groups of dancers. Their earliest films were '42nd Street', 'Gold Diggers of 1933', and 'Footlight Parade'.

Q. What were medieval buildings like?

A. Some of the best medieval architecture was seen in churches. Churches were built in two styles: Romanesque and Gothic. The Romanesque style used brick vaults and rounded arches. Gothic churches are tall with pointed-arch windows and doorways. They have beautiful stained-glass windows to let light in.

Q. Who were the gladiators?

A. The Romans in particular loved to watch sports where armed men and women, called gladiators, fought one another to death. Although some were professional, many were slaves forced to fight. Sometimes, they fought animals. Large stadiums were built for these games.

Q. Did ancient Man believe in religion?

A. There are signs that every ancient civilization believed in a higher power. The ancient Egyptians worshiped many gods and Egyptian Kings, called Pharaohs, were believed to be God's representatives on Earth. The ancient Mesopotamians, especially the Sumerians, had a strong belief in several gods who took human form.

Q. What is religion?

A. Religion is a set of rules based on faith in a spiritual power. It can also mean faith in plants, animals, ancestors and spirits. The word religion comes from the Latin noun 'religio', meaning rituals or faith. Most religions practiced today were started long ago.

Q. Which is the highest peak in South America?

A. The Aconcagua peak rises 6,960 metres (22,834 feet) in the Andes range in western Argentina. It is the highest peak in the western and southern hemispheres, and the highest in the world outside Asia.

Q. Where are the Great Lakes?

A. The Great Lakes include Superior, Huron, Erie and Ontario, on the border of Canada and the United States, and Lake Michigan in the USA. Together, these lakes make up the largest freshwater surface in the world.

Q. What languages are spoken in North America?

A. The United States has no official language but most people speak English and many speak Spanish too. In Canada, the two official languages are English and French. Spanish is the official language in Mexico.

Q. Where is Niagara Falls?

A. Niagara Falls is on the Niagara River, between Canada and the United States. It is actually three falls – the American Falls, the Bridal Veil Falls and the Canadian or Horseshoe Falls. In one minute, more than 168,000 cubic metres (6 million cubic feet) of water falls over its crest.

Q. Which is the highest waterfall in South America?

A. Angel Falls on Auyan Tepui river in Venezuela falls 979 metres (3,212 feet). It is the highest waterfall in the world. It is named after James Crawford Angel, who first saw it from his aeroplane in 1933. The local name is Churún Merú, which means Devil's Mouth.

Q. Which is the longest mountain range in South America?

A. Stretching for 7,000 kilometres (4,400 miles), the Andes is the longest mountain range in the world. It starts near the equator and goes on almost Antarctica. In some places, it is 500 kilometres (300 miles) wide.

Q. How crowded is Australia?

A. Australia is the sixth largest country in the world, but it has the lowest population density, with only two people living in every square kilometre.

Q. What is special about Australian sheep?

A. Australia has more than 101 million sheep! Most of them are merinos which produce an excellent light wool. They give us more than 70 per cent of the world's wool.

Q. What is a dingo?

A. The dingo is a wild dog of Australia. The dingo fence, which keeps sheep safe from dingoes, is the longest continuous fence in the world. It is 1.8 metres (5.9 feet) high and runs through Queensland for 5,531 kilometres (3,437 miles).

Q. What is special about Hawaii?

A. Except for Easter Island in the South Pacific, Hawaii is farthest from any other body of land. These volcanic islands are still expanding as more lava pours into the seabed.

Q. Is the Vatican City a country?

A. Vatican City, which is an enclave in Rome, is the world's smallest independent country. It is the seat of the Roman Catholic Church and is ruled by the Pope.

Q. Why is Norway called the 'Land of the Midnight Sun'?

A. One-third of Norway lies north of the Arctic Circle. From May to the end of July, this region has continuous daylight.

Q. Where is Istanbul?

A. Istanbul is in north-west Turkey. It is the only city in the world to be in two continents – Europe and Asia. It is divided into two by the Bosporus Strait.

Q. Is the Sahara the only desert in Africa?

A. Three major deserts cover one quarter of Africa. The Sahara covers 11 countries. The Kalahari desert and the Namib desert are in the south.

Q. Which is the highest point in Africa?

A. Kibo on Mount Kilimanjaro is the highest peak. It is 5,895 metres (19,341 feet) tall. Although close to the equator, the peak is so high that it is covered with snow.

Q. Does Africa have any big lakes?

A. Lakes Victoria, Tanganyika, Albert, Edward and Kivu are the Great Lakes of Africa, in the Great Rift Valley. Lake Victoria covers 69,500 square kilometres (26,836 square miles) and is the world's second largest freshwater lake.

Q. Does Africa have any big rivers?

A. The Nile River, at 6,825 kilometres (4,241 miles) long, is the longest river in the world. Other rivers in Africa include the Congo, the Zambezi and the Niger.

Q. Which are Asia's largest cities?

A. Seoul, Mumbai, Jakarta, Tokyo and Shanghai are some of the largest cities, not only in Asia, but in the world too!

Q. What languages are spoken in Asia?

A. There are more languages spoken in Asia than on any other continent – over 100 in the Philippines and more than 500 in Indonesia alone. Chinese, Hindi, Arabic and Bengali are among the languages spoken by over 100 million people. Chinese will soon be spoken by more people than any other language. People in most Asian countries speak more than one language.

Q. Why is June 21st an important day around the Arctic Circle?

A. On June 21st, or the summer solstice, the Sun does not set north of the Arctic Circle. That is why this area is called the Land of the Midnight Sun. For the local residents, this is a time to celebrate. On the other hand, on December 21st – the winter solstice – the Sun does not rise at all.

Q. What are the most famous architectural structures in Asia?

A. There are old cities, forts and monuments all over Asia. The Great Wall of China is the only man-made structure that can be seen from the moon! The Taj Mahal in India and Angkor Wat in Cambodia are among Asia's most famous monuments.

Q. What lies below the ice and snow at the Poles?

A. Many minerals have been found in the Arctic, although mining is difficult. Russia and the US have found deposits of coal, copper, nickel, gold, uranium, tungsten, diamonds, natural gas and oil. Antarctica may also be rich in minerals.

Q. Do people live in the Arctic?

A. Hunters from Siberia were the first people to live in the Arctic, arriving about 5,000 years ago. The Inuit of North America, the Greenlanders, the Lapps of Western Europe, and some groups of people in Russia and Siberia live in the Arctic. They hunt, fish and keep herds of reindeer.

Q. When did fish first evolve?

A. Fish first made an appearance over 500 million years ago. They developed over the next 100 million years to become fierce predators growing up to 10 metres (33 feet) long!

Q. What are the different ages in which life formed?

A. Life began in the Precambrian age. Then came the Palaeozoic age, which saw the first plants, most invertebrates, the first vertebrates, fish, amphibians, and reptiles. The Mesozoic age or the Age of Reptiles was when dinosaurs ruled the Earth. This was also when flowering plants, birds, and some mammals developed. Humans only appeared much later, in the Cenozoic period.

Q. How have scientists learned about the prehistoric world?

A. Many prehistoric creatures were fossilized in places such as tar pits. The creatures got stuck in the tar and died, leaving them completely preserved for millions of years.

Q. What was the first life form on Earth?

A. All life formed from tiny life forms called bacteria around 4.5 billion years ago.

Q. Is there any new clue as to how life began?

A. Scientists have found some animals among the mixture of gases that come out of volcanoes. Much of Earth was like this when life began. Therefore, any animal that can live here may hold a clue to the origin of life on Earth.

Q. Which was the biggest prehistoric fish?

A. At just under 30 metres in length, leedsichthys was not only the biggest fish of its time, it was the biggest fish of all time!

Q. When did plants start to grow?

A. The first plants appeared on earth over 400 million years ago. One of the earliest plants was cooksonia, which did not have leaves or flowers!

Q. How long have crocodiles been around?

A. The early ancestors of the crocodile, the sarcosuchus, lived over 100 million years ago and would have preyed on dinosaurs.

Q. Why is the colecanth called a living fossil?

A. The colecanth is one of the earliest known fossils that has survived until today. It grows to a length of 2 metres (6.5 feet). It was thought to be extinct until a fisherman off the coast of South Africa caught one in 1938.

Q. When did reptiles evolve?

A. Reptiles evolved around 70 million years after the first creature lived on land. Gradually, they adapted to living on land and grew from small reptiles into fierce dinosaurs.

Q. What did the dinosaurs eat?

A. Despite their reputation as violent monsters, 65 per cent of the dinosaurs were vegetarian. They lived around the same time as the first flowering plants were developing on the Earth. But most of the plants around them were like ferns. Some types of dinosaurs, such as the turanoceratops, had special parrot-like beaks with which they could bite off the needles from ferns.

Q. **What was the biggest land animal before the dinosaurs?**

A. Dimetrodon stalked the earth around 270 million years ago. It grew up to 3.5 metres (11.5 feet) and had a large fin on its back.

Q. **What was the biggest dinosaur of all?**

A. Experts are not certain, but argentinosaurus, seismosaurus and sauroposeidon were the largest at up to 35 metres (115 feet) and weighing over 60,000 kilograms (66 tons).

Q. **Why were the meat-eating dinosaurs special?**

A. Most meat-eating dinosaurs were smaller than their prey! But they were faster, with bigger and stronger jaws, sharp teeth and deadly claws that could kill and then tear apart the thick skin of another dinosaur.

Q. **Why is the tyrannosaurus rex so famous?**

A. Tyrannosaurus rex, also known as T-rex, was one of the largest meat-eating dinosaurs. It could stand up to a height of 12 metres (40 feet). It weighed between 5 and 7 tons - that's five to seven times the weight of the average elephant!

Q. **What was unique about maiasauras?**

A. Maiasauras were duck-billed, plant-eating dinosaurs that lived in herds of 10,000 or more. Unlike all the other dinosaurs, maiasauras were believed to have looked after their offspring in much the same manner as modern mammals.

Q. What did the stegosaurus use the plates on its back for?

A. Stegosaurus probably used its plates to scare away its enemies. Many scientists think these plates also helped the dinosaur to regulate its body temperature.

Q. How big were the plates on the stegosaurus?

A. The largest plates on the back of a stegosaurus were at least 60 centimetres (2 feet) tall and wide.

Q. How big were the flying dinosaurs?

A. The largest flying dinosaur was quetzalcoatlus, which had a wingspan of around 12 metres (40 feet). That's four times bigger than today's largest bird, the albatross.

Q. Do we know about every dinosaur that lived?

A. It is unlikely – around forty per cent of all known dinosaurs were only discovered within the last 20 years.

Q. Why aren't dinosaurs around today?

A. Dinosaurs disappeared from earth around 65 million years ago. Around fifty per cent of all life was wiped out and experts today still do not know for certain why.

Q. Were there any prehistoric flightless birds?

A. Phorusrhacos was a fierce giant bird that could not fly. It stood 2.5 metres (8.2 feet) tall and some adults probably weighed over 130 kilograms (287 pounds). It was one of the largest birds ever.

Q. What is a glyptodont?

A. Glyptodont was one of the earliest forms of the armadillo. These curious animals weighed over 1,000 kilograms (2,200 pounds) and their body was covered with armour about 5 centimetres (2 inches) thick.

Q. When did sauropods live?

A. Sauropods were plentiful during the Triassic and Jurassic periods. Very few of these gigantic creatures survived into the Cretaceous period.

Q. What is a brontotherium?

A. Brontotherium means 'thunder animal'. It was a large mammal similar to a rhinoceros, with a forked horn on its snout. Many fossils of this animal have been found in South Dakota and Nebraska in the USA. Often, they were found after the soil covering the fossil had been washed away by a big rainstorm. That is how the prehistoric beast came to be known as the thunder animal.

Q. When did the first humans appear?

A. The oldest human remains found so far come from Africa and are nearly 6 million years old. They show that humans originally looked a lot like apes and even spent time climbing up trees!

Q. When did modern humans evolve?

A. Our own direct relatives – Homo sapiens – have only been around for the last 130,000 years.

Planet Earth

Q. How big is the Grand Canyon?

A. The Grand Canyon is about 446 kilometres (277 miles)
long and roughly 1.6 kilometres (1 mile) deep.
It is made up of several layers of rock,
each one older than the one above it.

Q. Why is the ozone layer important?

A. The ozone layer is important because it stops harmful ultraviolet rays from the Sun from reaching the Earth. If the rays are allowed through the atmosphere, they can cause severe health problems like skin cancer. Chemicals called CFCs have made a hole in the ozone layer above the North and South Poles.

Q. Does the Sun really rise in the east?

A. The Earth spins in an eastward direction. This makes the Sun appear as if it is rising in the east and setting in the west.

Q. What causes day and night?

A. The Earth turning on its axis is responsible for day and night. At any time, half the Earth faces the Sun, where it is day, and half faces away, where it is night.

Q. What is the Coriolis effect?

A. The wind moves to the right in the northern hemisphere and to the left in the southern hemisphere. This is called the Coriolis effect. It is caused by the Earth's rotation. It is mainly responsible for thunderstorms and hurricanes.

Q. What is a barometer?

A. A barometer is used to measure the pressure in the atmosphere. When the pressure is high, the weather will be fine, sunny and still. When it is low, the weather will be stormy. When the pressure increases the liquid in the barometer is squeezed and when the pressure decreases it is released. This change is recorded.

Q. Why are days longer in summer and shorter in winter?

A. The angle at which sunlight falls on a particular area determines the length of day and night in that region. During summer, the Sun stays above the horizon longer, making the days longer.

Q. How are glacial valleys formed?

A. When glaciers slowly flow downhill, they collect many pieces of rock on the way. These pieces scrape against the valley floor, digging deeper into it, until a U-shaped valley is formed.

Q. What causes an ocean current?

A. An ocean current is a mass of water that keeps moving in one direction. Surface currents are caused by wind and the Earth's rotation. Underwater currents are the result of differences in temperature and salt content of the water.

Q. What is a black smoker?

A. When water seeps into the crust of the ocean floor through cracks, it is heated by the magma below. As pressure builds up within the crust, the hot water shoots up through the cracks. These jets of warm water are often black due to their mineral content, so they are called black smokers.

Q. What are geysers?

A. Geysers are jets of hot water that erupt from the Earth. When water trickles down into the hot molten rock under the Earth's crust, it is heated up. As the water becomes hotter, the pressure builds up, finally causing it to spurt out.

Q. Can we predict earthquakes?

A. The movements of the Earth are too complex for us to be able to predict earthquakes. But we do know the lines along which the Earth's plates meet, so we know the areas that are more likely to have earthquakes.

Q. What is liquefaction?

A. Liquefaction is caused by the violent shaking of the ground during an earthquake. Moist soil or sand turns into slurry, like quicksand. This liquid can suck in entire buildings.

Q. Which is the highest volcano on Earth?

A. Mauna Loa in Hawaii is the highest volcano on Earth. It is about 4 kilometres (2.5 miles) above sea level; below that, it extends to 5 kilometres (3.1 miles) down before it reaches the seabed. Then, its massive weight has pushed the volcano down a further 8 kilometres (5 miles) below the seabed! So Mauna Loa is 17 kilometres (10.5 miles) from its base to its summit.

Q. Can hurricane winds be measured?

A. Hurricanes are divided into five categories depending on their wind speeds. Category five hurricanes are the worst, causing maximum damage. Winds of a category five hurricane can reach speeds of about 250 kilometres (155 miles) per hour. Category one hurricanes are much weaker, and only travel at 119–153 kilometres per hour (74–95 miles per hour).

Q. How did tornadoes get their name?

A. The word tornado is from the Spanish word tomear, meaning 'to turn'.

Q. What is the Fujita scale?

A. The Fujita scale is used to measure the intensity of a tornado. It ranks tornadoes by the damage caused to man-made structures.

Q. Is a tsunami the same as a tidal wave?

A. A tsunami is different from a tidal wave. A tidal wave is generated by high winds, but a tsunami is caused by underwater earthquakes, landslides or volcanic eruptions.

Q. Which is the highest mountain peak in the world?

A. At a height of about 8,848 metres (29,028 feet) above sea level, Mount Everest is the highest peak in the world. It is a part of the Himalayan mountain range that was formed about 10–15 million years ago.

Q. Which is the largest freshwater lake in the world?

A. Lake Superior, one of the Great Lakes of North America, is the largest freshwater lake in the world. This lake is over 560 kilometres (350 miles) long and about 257 kilometres (160 miles) wide.

Q. What is an avalanche?

A. An avalanche is a very large sudden slide of snow, ice or rocks down a mountainside or cliff.

Q. Which is the largest of all oceans?

A. The Pacific Ocean is the world's largest and deepest ocean. It has an average depth of more than 4,000 metres (13,100 feet). It also has the world's deepest trench – the Mariana Trench off the coast of Japan. The Challenger Deep in the Mariana Trench is the deepest point on Earth – about 11,033 metres (36,200 feet) below ground level.

Q. Which is the most active volcano?

A. Mount St. Helens in Washington State of USA is the most active volcano. It last erupted in 1980.

Q. Why is Lake Baikal special?

A. Lake Baikal in southern Siberia is the deepest lake in the world, with a maximum depth of 1,637 metres (5,371 feet). It has been around for almost 30 million years.

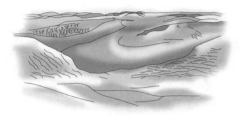

Q. What is the Sahara known for?

A. The Sahara is the largest hot desert in the world. Located in Africa, it spreads across Mauritania, Morocco, Mali, Algeria, Tunisia, Niger, Libya, Chad, Egypt, Sudan and Eritrea.

Q. What was the worst earthquake in history?

A. In 1556, an earthquake struck three provinces in China. About 830,000 people were killed in the disaster. It was the most destructive earthquake ever recorded.

Q. What is a storm surge?

A. Sometimes the strong winds of a hurricane can cause the water level in the ocean to rise. Huge waves hit the coast along with the storm, causing severe flooding. This is called a storm surge.

Q. What is the exosphere?

A. The exosphere is the outer layer of the Earth's atmosphere. It extends way into space. The air in the exosphere is very thin, but the temperature is very high, because the Sun's rays shine directly into it.

Science and Technology

Q. What color is light?

A. Light usually appears white, but is made up of various colors of the rainbow: red, orange, yellow, green, blue, indigo and violet (ROYGBIV).

Q. Can I look at an atom?

A. You cannot look at an atom directly, even through the most powerful optical microscopes, because atoms are much smaller than the wavelengths of light that optical microscopes detect. A human hair is as wide as one million carbon atoms. However, we can detect the position of an atom on the surface of a solid with an electron microscope, so we know it is there.

Q. What is a light year?

A. A light year is the distance that light travels in a year.

Q. Why does the Sun look like a red disc during sunrise and sunset?

A. During sunrise and sunset, the sunlight has to travel a much longer distance than during the rest of the day. The scattered blue light is not able to cover this extra distance and therefore does not reach our eyes. The red light reaches us, as the wavelength of red is longer. This helps red light travel further. This is why the Sun appears like a red disc.

Q. How do we speak?

A. Human beings have vocal chords inside the larynx which produce sound. When air passes through a gap between the chords, these chords vibrate and produce a sound. All animals that can produce sound have vocal chords, except birds which produce sound through a bony ring, called a syrinx.

Q. Why do things expand when heated?

A. When you heat solids, liquids or gases, they expand because the molecules start moving faster. To move fast, they need more space, so they expand.

Q. When was the first artificial satellite launched?

A. Sputnik 1 was launched by the then USSR on October 4th, 1957. It reached a height of about 250 kilometres (150 miles) and collected information about the farthest reaches of the Earth's atmosphere. Three months later, it burned up completely as it came back to Earth.

Q. Who owns the satellites in space?

A. The first satellites were owned by countries. Today, with satellites becoming cheaper and doing more work, companies also own satellites. The area on the surface of the Earth covered by the satellite's signal is called its 'footprint'.

Q. What is a constellation?

A. Groups of satellites doing the same kind of work are called a constellation. The Global Positioning System is one such constellation made up of twenty-four satellites. GPS works in any weather condition, anywhere in the world, 24 hours a day. A GPS instrument can tell you exactly where you are on Earth.

Q. **What is thermodynamics?**

A. Thermodynamics is the study of heat and how it can help us.

Q. **What do the words 'opaque' and 'transparent' mean?**

A. Solids are said to be opaque, as they do not allow light to pass through them, while water and glass are transparent as light is able to pass through.

Q. **What is a super atom?**

A. When some elements are cooled to a temperature just above absolute zero, the atoms begin to clump together to become one 'super atom'. Super atoms have only been made in laboratories for a fraction of a second.

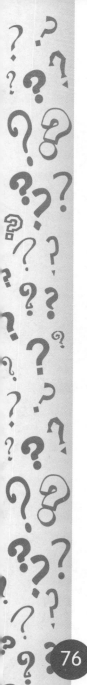

Q. What is boiling point?

A. The temperature at which a substance changes from liquid to gas is called its boiling point. The melting point of a substance is the temperature at which it changes from solid to liquid.

Q. What are good conductors of heat?

A. Metals are the best conductors of heat. That is why cooking pans are made of metal to carry the heat from the stove to the pan. Wood and plastic are poor conductors. That is why the handles of cooking utensils are often made of these materials, so that we don't burn our hands!

Q. How does ultrasonic sound help doctors?

A. Ultrasonic sound waves help doctors locate and diagnose medical problems, because different tissues reflect sound waves in different ways. Using this method, doctors can also monitor the development of a foetus during pregnancy.

Q. What is the range of sound that the human ear can hear?

A. A young human being can hear almost all sounds from 15 Hz to 20,000 Hz. With age, we hear less, and find it difficult to catch higher frequencies. A human voice carries sound at about 60 Hz, but a shout can reach 13,000 Hz. Elephants, dogs and other animals can hear ultrasonic sound that we cannot.

Q. What is net force?

A. When more than one force acts on an object, the total of all forces acting on that object is called the net force. When more than one force acts on an object in the same direction, the object moves faster. If the forces act in opposing directions, they cancel each other out to a certain extent.

Q. How do power stations generate so much electricity?

A. Power stations convert the kinetic energy of moving water (hydroelectricity); heat produced by burning coal (thermal electricity) or a nuclear reaction (nuclear power); the kinetic energy of wind (wind power) that turns a windmill; tide movements (tidal power); or heat from inside the Earth (geothermal power) to generate electricity.

Q. Why do things stick only to the poles of a magnet?

A. Magnets are strongest at their poles so objects stick to the poles most easily.

Q. Are magnets strong forever?

A. Magnets get weaker with time. The best way to store them is to keep them in pairs with the unlike poles next to each other and placing keepers or pieces of soft iron across the ends. The keepers become temporary magnets themselves and keep the magnetic force stronger.

Q. What is an electromagnet?

A. Winding an electric wire around a piece of iron can make electromagnets. When electric current runs through the wire, a magnetic field is created. The iron piece picks this up and becomes a magnet.

Q. How can you destroy a magnet?

A. Though magnets can be natural or manmade, dropping, heating or hammering them can destroy them, especially if they are small and weak.

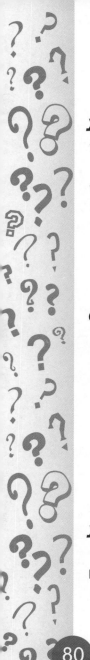

Q. What is lateral deflection?

A. This is a force that makes a bullet spin to one side, or a football curl through the air. During the Soccer World Cup in France in 1998, Brazilian Roberto Carlos scored a free kick with a perfect lateral deflection. He kicked the ball to the far right of the defenders and made it suddenly curve round and zoom into the goal.

Q. If electricity lights a bulb, does it also light my torch?

A. A bulb is lit with electricity from a power generator. Another source of electricity is the battery. It has chemicals that react and produce a small amount of electricity, just enough for a torch.

Q. Who was the first person to sail around the world single-handedly?

A. American seaman Joshua Slocum was the first man to sail around the world single-handedly. He started off from Boston on April 24th 1895, and returned to Newport, Rhode Island on June 27th 1898, having sailed 74,000 kilometres (46,000 miles) in over three years.

Q. When was the wheel invented?

A. Mesopotamians invented the wheel as early as the fifth century 3500 BC. At first it was used to make pottery but later people realized that wheels could be attached to carts and used to move things and people easily.

Q. When were the first cars produced in a factory?

A. In 1896, 13 Dureyas cars were made in a factory in Springfield, Massachusetts (USA). These were the very first examples of mass-produced cars.

Q. What are modern ships made of?

A. Boats and ships continued to be made of wood for centuries. With the start of the Industrial Revolution, people began to use steel to build ships. Today, ships are also made of aluminium and fibreglass.

Q. What is the record speed for land travel?

A. The latest record speed for land travel was achieved on October 15th, 1997 by Andy Green of Britain in a Thrust SSC car. He travelled at a speed of 1,233.738 kilometres (766.609 miles) per hour!

Q. What is a seaplane?

A. Seaplanes, developed by Glenn H. Curtiss, can land on and take off from the surface of water. They are useful for reaching areas where no other transport is available. There are two types of seaplanes: floatplanes are planes with large floats instead of wheels; flying boats are planes that float on their bellies when they land.

Q. How does a hovercraft work?

A. A hovercraft can travel on water and land. It stays suspended a few centimetres above the ground or water surface with the help of an air cushion that it creates by the thrust of its jet engines. It is used as a fast patrol boat by the police and military of several countries and also for watersports.

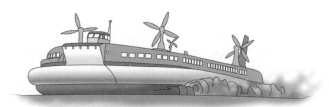

Q. What was the Concorde?

A. In the 1960s, jets that could travel faster than the speed of sound were developed. These were called supersonic jets. The Concorde was a commercial supersonic jet which could fly at a height of 17,500 metres (60,000 feet) at more than twice the speed of sound.

Q. What are airships?

A. Airships were among the earliest aircrafts. They were filled with hydrogen gas or helium, which helped them to float. Engine-driven airships, called Zeppelins, were widely used by Germany in World War I to launch bombing attacks on enemy territory. Today, flexible airships are used in advertising.

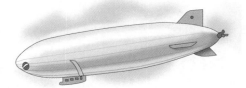

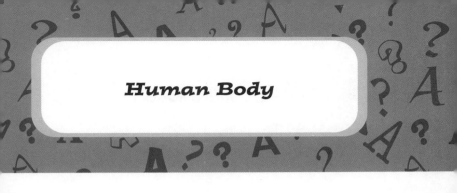

Human Body

Q. What hair on the body grows the quickest?

A. Facial hair is the quickest growing hair on the body. If a man never cuts his beard, it would grow to more than 9 metres (29.5 feet) long!

Q. What is a lunula?

A. The lunula is a crescent of pale skin
at the base of the nails.

Q. What role does the tongue play in digestion?

A. The tongue has millions of tiny taste buds that help us
to identify whether the food is salty, bitter, sweet or sour.

Q. How long does it take a nail to grow?

A. On an average, nails grow 2.5 millimetres (0.1 inches)
in a month. It takes one nail cell 3–6 months to grow from
the bottom to the tip of the finger.

Q. How much skin do we have?

A. An adult has more than two square metres (20 square feet) of skin. This is almost the size of a bed sheet!

Q. Does our skin last forever?

A. No – skin cells die and are replaced every day. Every minute of your life over 30,000 skin cells drop off your body to form dust.

Q. What is the sweatiest part of the body?

A. Contrary to belief, the underarms are not the sweatiest part of the body; it is the palms of your hands, followed by your feet!

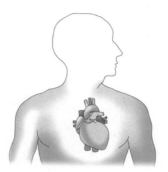

Q. How many times does the heart beat?

A. The heart beats about 100,000 times in one day. It begins beating from before a child is born and does not stop until the person dies.

Q. Why does my stomach rumble when I'm hungry?

A. This sound is the result of the stomach churning around half-digested food, gas and acid.

Q. How long does food stay in the stomach?

A. Food can take up to four hours to be digested by the stomach. This is only the beginning of the process – it can take up to two days for food to pass through the body completely.

Q. What is the alimentary canal?

A. The alimentary canal, also called the digestive tract, is a long tube that starts at the mouth and ends at the anus. It includes organs, such as the stomach, small and large intestines, and rectum.

Q. What does the pancreas do?

A. The pancreas is located behind the stomach. This organ releases chemicals that help break down proteins, fats and carbohydrates. It also helps maintain sugar levels in the body and prevents diabetes.

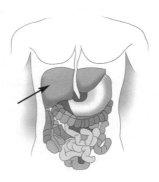

Q. How does the liver work?

A. The liver is not part of the digestive tract, but it plays a vital role in digestion. It releases a substance called bile that helps to break down fat. The liver also stores excess fat for later use.

Q. Does everyone have the same kind of blood?

A. There are different types of human blood, so it has been divided into four groups – A, B, AB and O. Most people have a blood protein called rhesus factor. This makes their blood positive. People who do not have this protein have rhesus negative blood.

Q. What is blood?

A. Blood is sometimes called 'the river of life' and it accounts for about eight per cent of our weight. Blood contains two types of blood cells: red and white. Both types are suspended in a fluid called plasma. Vitamins and minerals from food are distributed in the body by blood.

Q. What is bone marrow?

A. Bone marrow is the soft tissue inside our bones. It produces blood cells. Since red blood cells only live for about 120 days and white blood cells only for a few days, the bone marrow works constantly.

Q. Are we born with all our bones in our body?

A. Babies are born without kneecaps – these develop between two to six years of age.

Q. How many eggs does a woman have?

A. The ovaries hold thousands of eggs. These are released once a month for about 30 years during menstruation. When a woman is between 45 to 50 years old, menstruation stops and eggs are no longer released. This change is called the menopause.

Q. For how many years can the male reproductive system produce sperm?

A. Unlike females, males can produce sperm throughout their life. However, their fertility declines with age.

Q. What is a bruise?

A. A bruise is bleeding under your skin. It cannot leave the body if there is no cut, so it leaks around the affected area. Bruises are purple because that is the colour of blood when it has no oxygen.

Q. How long can I go without sleeping?

A. The average person needs eight hours sleep a night. Going without sleep for two weeks can be enough to kill you!

Q. Why do we have to sleep?

A. Similar to machines, it is essential for humans to 'switch off' and repair themselves at night. When you are asleep your body is busy healing wounds and replacing dead skin cells much more quickly than when you are awake.

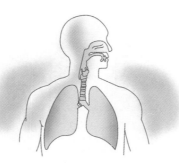

Q. How many tubes does the throat have?

A. The throat consists of two tubes – one for food, and one for air. A small flap called an epiglottis closes the windpipe the moment we swallow, preventing food from entering the windpipe.

Q. Why is it important to chew food?

A. The more we chew the easier it is for the body to digest food. As we chew, the mouth releases saliva that moistens the food so that it passes through the digestive system without scraping any of the organs.

Q. Why do we sometimes choke on our food?

A. Sometimes food accidentally enters the windpipe, causing us to choke. This usually happens when we laugh or talk while eating, or swallow food without chewing properly.

Q. What is the circulatory system?

A. The heart, the lungs and the blood vessels are part of the circulatory system. Humans have about 100,000 kilometres (62,000 miles) of blood vessels in their body. This is enough to circle the Earth two and a half times! Blood vessels are made up of arteries, veins and capillaries.

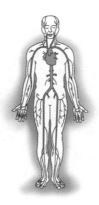

Q. **Are there more red blood cells than white ones?**

A. Red blood cells make up about 45 per cent of our
blood. There is only one white blood cell for every
600 red blood cells.

Q. **What is the difference between red and
white blood cells?**

A. Red blood cells give blood its colour and also help to
carry carbon dioxide and oxygen to and from the lungs.
White blood cells help to fight infection and they also help
the blood to clot if we are wounded.

Q. What makes up the central nervous system?

A. The brain, millions of nerves and the spinal cord make up the central nervous system of the human body. All the information gathered by sense organs like the eyes, ears, nose, tongue and skin is processed in the brain.

Q. How do we actually see?

A. We see through our eyes, but it is due to our brain that we know we are seeing this page and not something else. When light enters our eyes, special nerves inside the eyes carry a message to the brain. Then the brain understands what we are seeing.

Q. **What are germs?**

A. Germs are tiny creatures visible only through a microscope. These include bacteria and viruses. Harmful bacteria cause infections like sore throats and stomach upsets. Viruses can cause chickenpox, measles and influenza. We catch germs from people who are unwell, from unhygienic food or water, or from our surroundings.

Q. **How many hair follicles do I have?**

A. The head has about 100,000 hair follicles and the body has about five million.

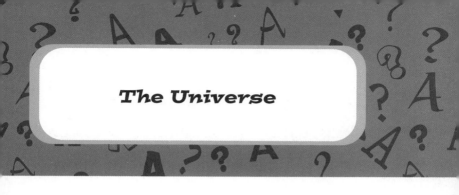

Q. How many stars are there in the universe?

A. We know of about 70 sextillion (7 followed by 22 zeros) stars in the universe. However, we are only able to see about 8,000 of these.

Q. What is the Big Bang theory?

A. The Big Bang theory suggests that the universe as we know it today was created after a huge explosion or 'bang'. Georges Lemaitre proposed the theory of the Big Bang in 1927, and in 1929 Edwin Hubble expanded on his work.

Q. Which is the largest galaxy?

A. Scientists do not know exactly. The largest galaxies we know of are giant elliptical (oval) galaxies located in the middle of a whole group of galaxies. One of the largest is in the central galaxy in the cluster Abell 2029.

Q. How big is the Milky Way?

A. The Milky Way is huge! It takes the Sun about 250 million years to orbit once around the centre of the Milky Way.

Q. **What is Messier Object 31?**

A. The Andromeda Galaxy is also known as Messier Object 31, or M31. This galaxy is more than twice the size of the Milky Way, but it is still not the largest galaxy we know of.

Q. **What are giant and dwarf stars?**

A. Scientists classify stars as giant or dwarf stars on the basis of their size. The Sun is a dwarf star. Supergiant stars – the biggest in the universe – are at least 400 times bigger than the Sun.

Q. **Which is the brightest known star?**

A. The Pistol Star is the brightest known star in the universe. It is about ten million times brighter than the Sun.

Q. What kind of stars are binary stars?

A. Pairs of stars are called binary stars. Binary stars revolve around the same centre of gravity.

Q. What are sunspots?

A. Sunspots are storms on the surface of the Sun. These storms appear as huge, dark spots in satellite pictures and so are called sunspots.

Q. What is a cluster of stars?

A. Stars are usually found in groups called clusters. Some clusters are made up of loosely packed stars, while other stars are packed tightly together to form a dense cluster.

Q. How hot is the Sun?

A. The Sun's surface temperature is about 5,760 °C (10,400 °F), while its centre is an incredible 15 million °C (28 million °F) – that's more than 150,000 times hotter than boiling water!

Q. How far is the Sun from Earth?

A. The Sun is about 150 million kilometres (93 million miles) away from the Earth.

Q. What is the corona?

A. The corona is the glowing atmosphere of the Sun that extends millions of kilometres into space. The corona is 200 times hotter than the Sun's surface.

Q. Is the Sun worshipped by people?

A. The Sun has been worshipped as a god since ancient times by the Greeks, Romans and Native Americans.

Q. If the Moon is cold and dark, how does it give off light?

A. The Moon does not give off light of its own. It simply reflects the sunlight that falls on it.

Q. Why can't we see the Moon during the day?

A. During the day the bright light of the Sun blocks the soft glow of light reflected by the Moon.

Q. Does our Moon have a scientific name?

A. Astronomers call the Earth's moon Luna, to distinguish it from the natural satellites of other planets.

Q. What are sungrazers?

A. Some comets crash into the Sun or get so close to it that they break up into tiny pieces. Such comets are called sungrazers.

Q. What are spring tides and neap tides?

A. When the Sun, the Moon and the Earth are in a straight line, the gravitational force of the Sun strengthens that of the Moon, causing tides that are higher than usual. These are called spring tides (although they have nothing to do with the season of Spring). When the Sun and the Moon are at right angles to the Earth, weaker tides, called neap tides, occur. Tides are important to wash away the debris off the coasts.

Q. Where are asteroids found in the solar system?

A. Most asteroids are found in a region between Mars and Jupiter, which is known as the asteroid belt.

Q. Do asteroids have moons?

A. The asteroid Ida has a tiny moon, Dactyl. This was discovered by the spacecraft Galileo in 1993.

Q. **Why does a comet have a tail?**

A. A comet is made up of ice and other material. As it nears the Sun, these materials heat up. Solar wind and pressure from the Sun's radiation push them outwards to form a tail that always points away from the Sun.

Q. **When will Halley's Comet be seen again?**

A. Halley's Comet takes about 76 years to complete one orbit around the Sun, so it is expected to be seen again in 2061.

Q. How did the planets get their names?

A. All the planets are named after Roman gods. Venus, for example, is named after the Roman goddess of love. The surface features of Venus are also named after various goddesses, with a deep canyon named Diana, after the Roman goddess of hunting.

Q. How many moons does Venus have?

A. Venus and Mercury are the only planets in the solar system that have no moon.

Q. What about Pluto?

A. Until recently, Pluto was the ninth planet in our solar system. But in 2006, it was officially reclassified as a dwarf planet, because it is so small and its gravitational field is not as strong as that of the major planets.

Q. How long does Mercury take to orbit the Sun?

A. Like all planets, Mercury goes around the Sun in an elliptical (oval) orbit. It takes about 88 days to complete one orbit.

Q. How long is a day on Mercury?

A. Mercury goes around the Sun very fast, but rotates very slowly on its axis. Therefore a day on Mercury is equal to 176 Earth days!

Q. Why does Mercury have huge craters?

A. As Mercury has very little atmosphere, meteors do not burn up in the air. Instead, they fall on the surface, creating huge craters.

Q. What color is the sky above Mercury?

A. If you were to look at the sky from Mercury, even during the day, it would appear black. This is because there is no atmosphere to spread the Sun's light.

Q. Which is the largest crater on Mercury?

A. The largest crater is the Caloris Basin. It is about 1,300 kilometres (808 miles) in diameter. It is also one of the biggest craters in the solar system.

Q. Who discovered Uranus?

A. Uranus was the first planet to be seen through a telescope. It was discovered in 1781 by astronomer William Herschel.

Q. How many rings do Jupiter and Uranus have?

A. Jupiter has three thin rings that cannot be seen even with the most powerful telescopes. Uranus has as many as 11 rings.

Q. Can you see Mars from Earth?

A. On a clear night, Mars can be observed with the naked eye. Between July and September, the Martian surface can be observed clearly through a telescope.

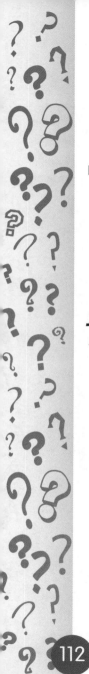

Q. How many moons does Mars have?

A. Mars has two moons called Phobos and Deimos, which orbit very closely to its surface. Both moons are believed to be asteroids that were captured by the gravity of Mars as they came close to it.

Q. Is there life on Mars?

A. The atmosphere of Mars is 95 per cent carbon dioxide, 3 percent nitrogen and 1.6 per cent argon. Traces of oxygen and water have also been found. Some scientists have claimed to have found traces of methane. This gave rise to the speculation that there may be life on Mars, since methane is a gas produced by many animals. But other scientists pointed out that methane is also produced by the mineral olivine, which can also be found on Mars.

Q. When were Saturn's rings discovered?

A. Saturn's rings were first observed by Galileo Galilei through a telescope in 1610.

Q. How big are Saturn's rings?

A. Saturn's rings can be up to one kilometre (0.6 miles) thick and stretch for over 280,000 kilometres (175,000 miles).

Q. What was the first living being to orbit Earth?

A. The first creature to orbit the Earth was a dog named Laika, aboard the Russian spacecraft Sputnik 2 on November 3rd, 1957.

Q. Which was the first ever space station?

A. Salyut 1 was the first space station. It was launched on April 19th, 1971.

Q. Who was the first person in space?

A. On 12 April 1961, Russian cosmonaut Yuri Gagarin was the first person to travel in space, aboard the spacecraft Vostok 1. Gagarin orbited the Earth once on this historic flight, which lasted 1 hour and 48 minutes.

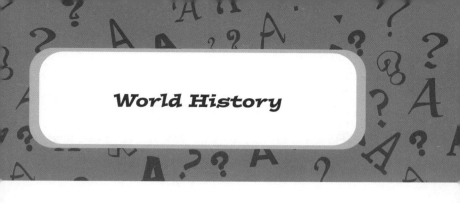

Q. What was special about the Colosseum?

A. The Colosseum is a huge open-air theatre in Rome. It was built by Emperor Vespasian and his sons. It held 50,000 people. Gladiatorial games and mock naval battles were the main events held in it.

Q. Were there wars in ancient Mesopotamia?

A. Mesopotamians fought with each other over land, water and power. The first ever war probably took place between the cities of Lagash and Umma.

Q. Which was the oldest Mesopotamian civilization?

A. The Sumerians settled in Mesopotamia about 4000 BC, making them the first civilization in the world.

Q. Who ruled Mesopotamia?

A. Every Mesopotamian city was ruled by a king, who was thought to have been chosen by the god of the city.

Q. What was the Oracle at Delphi?

A. In ancient Greece, Delphi was the site of the most important oracle. People would go to there for advice and to pray, as the oracle was a very wise person believed to be able to predict the future.

Q. Who was Homer?

A. Homer is one of the best-known Greek writers. He wrote the two famous epic poems – 'The Iliad' and 'The Odyssey'.

Q. Who were the bestiarii?

A. Sometimes, criminals who had been sentenced to death and prisoners of war were forced to fight wild animals with their bare hands in the Roman arena. They were called bestiarii.

Q. What does Mughal mean?

A. Mughal comes from the Persian word for Mongol. The first Mughal Emperor, Babur, was from a Mongol family.

Q. What are insulae?

A. The poor people in ancient Rome lived in small, crowded apartments known as insulae. These apartments had only two or three rooms and large families lived in them.

Q. Which was the first British colony to gain independence?

A. In 1776, 13 British colonies in North America signed the Declaration of Independence. They formed the United States of America.

Q. Who was Empress Xi Ling-Shi?

A. Empress Xi Ling-Shi is said to have discovered silk when a cocoon fell into her cup of tea and the silk unravelled. By 3000 BC, silk was worn by Chinese royalty.

Q. Did ancient Greeks know about democracy?

A. Democracy is a form of government where the people in power are elected by the citizens of a country. It originated in Athens.

Q. Did ancient Greeks make pottery?

A. Ancient Greeks made pottery for their daily use. Some of the most commonly used vessels included amphora (wine jars), hydria (water jars) and krater (mixing bowls). These vessels were often painted with beautiful scenes from famous Greek legends.

Q. What is Mohenjo-Daro?

A. Mohenjo-Daro was the largest city in the Indus Valley and means 'mound of the dead'. It had been abandoned for many centuries. Then in 1924, while a railway line was under construction, workers started digging near the mound. When archaeologists saw the ancient bricks the workers were digging up, they realized they had hit upon an important ancient site.

Q. Did all ancient Romans wear togas?

A. A toga was a long piece of cloth worn by men in ancient Rome. It was usually draped over the tunic. The toga was a symbol of the person's position in society. Therefore, slaves and most poor men did not wear togas.

Q. Why did the Mesoamericans bury jewellery with their dead?

A. The Mesoamericans believed in life after death. They buried their dead with jewellery, vases and toys they thought were needed in the afterlife. The Mayans believed that ordinary people went to the underworld when dead, but when kings died, they went to heaven and were reborn as kings in another world. They were buried in elaborate tombs.

Q. What type of gods did Mesoamericans believe in?

A. Ancient Mesoamerican gods were part human and part animal. They represented natural elements like the Sun and the Moon, rain, lightning and the planets.

Q. What is origami?

A. The Japanese perfected the art of folding paper into three-dimensional figures and shapes. Origami may have come to Japan with Buddhist monks from China. Others believe Origami is an art form that was developed in Japan. Only a few folds are used in Origami, but the folds can be combined in a variety of ways to make intricate designs. Most Origami designs begin with a square sheet that can be different colours on each side.

Q. Who discovered the cocoa that we all love?

A. The Maya loved to drink hot cocoa. They believed cocoa was a gift from their snake god Quetzalcoatl and that it could cure them of illness. Chocolate is made from cocoa.

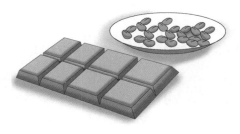

Q. What was a castle?

A. A castle was the home and fortress of a lord or king. They had ramparts from which soldiers could attack the enemy if the castle was besieged. Many people besides the lord or king lived in it, including servants, soldiers, cooks, blacksmiths and falconers. Cows, horses, pigs and chickens were also kept there for food.

Q. What was the Silk Route?

A. The Silk Route was an important trade route that began in China and ran across Central Asia, all the way to Europe. Silk was the cloth worn by royalty in China. This land route was important until the early sixteenth century.

Q. Did the Renaissance change music?

A. During the Renaissance, musicians learned many things about the science of sound waves, which helped them to create the kind of music they wanted. Composers studied Greek drama and were inspired to create opera.

Q. What was in fashion in Renaissance?

A. Women shaved or plucked off their eyebrows. Even the Mona Lisa has none!

Q. What did people wear?

A. Knights wore sleeveless coats decorated with their coat of arms. Rich men wore cloaks and rich women wore tunics that reached to their ankles. Married women tied their hair in a bun and wore tight caps and nets over it. Unmarried women could leave their hair loose or braided. Hair was an important indication of rank and status.

Q. What is the Taj Mahal?

A. The Mughals loved architecture. They built complicated and intricately decorated mosques, tombs and strong forts at Agra and Delhi. They also studied the science of landscaping and created beautiful gardens. Shah Jehan built the Taj Mahal as a tomb for his beloved wife, Mumtaz Mahal.

Q. Who were the navratnas?

A. Navratna means 'nine jewels' in the Hindi language. These were nine talented men in the court of Akbar. They included Tansen the singer, Todar Mal the administrator, Abul Fazl, the emperor's chief advisor and Maharaja Man Singh, Akbar's trusted general.

Q. Who was Mona Lisa?

A. The Mona Lisa is probably the most famous painting ever created and was painted by Leonardo da Vinci. The model is said to be Lisa Gherardini, who was the wife of a nobleman. The painting is in the Louvre, Paris.

Q. How did technology help improve sailing?

A. New gadgets made sailing more accurate and safe. The chronometer was a special clock that kept time even on rough seas. The compass helped the sailor find his way. The astrolabe helped predict the position of the Sun, Moon and stars, as well as tell the time.

Q. How did the Pacific Ocean get its name?

A. Ferdinand Magellan gave the Pacific Ocean its name, which means 'peaceful' or 'calm'. After battling through the fierce Cape Horn at the tip of South America, he found the Pacific Ocean unusually still.

Q. What did European explorers bring home with them?

A. The sailors brought riches and spices from the new lands. Foods like the potato, tomato and chilli were introduced. Animals like jaguars and tapirs, and birds like macaws and toucans were brought for the zoos of Europe. Many shipowners became very rich carrying gold and other treasures for the government.

Q. What was special about the colony in Australia?

A. Between 1788 and 1853, thousands of English criminals were shipped off to Australia because the English jails were too full. These were the first British settlers in Australia.

Q. Were there any passengers on the world's first balloon flight?

A. Yes - a sheep, a chicken and a duck. King Louis XVI of France watched them through his telescope.

Q. Who were the Vikings?

A. The Vikings came from the Scandinavian countries of Denmark, Norway and Sweden. Although some of them were fierce raiders, most were farmers, craftsmen and traders.

Q. When was the Viking Age?

A. The Viking Age began about 1200 years ago in the eighth century AD and lasted for about 300 years.